SERMON ON THE MOUNT

HE OPENED HIS MOUTH AND BEGAN TO TEACH THEM, SAYING...

Early in His ministry Jesus passed through the region of Galilee teaching in synagogues, preaching "the Gospel of the kingdom," and healing every kind of sickness. As news of these miracles spread rapidly to several other regions, people brought their desperately sick relatives and friends to Him. When He healed all of them, a huge crowd began to follow Him.

At a strategic point, He headed up a mountain overlooking the Sea of Galilee to teach them what has become known as the "Sermon on the Mount."

Now *what exactly* did He say that was so important to such a vast audience and to us today?

You'll discover *what* in these ten programs:

1. Who the religious authorities in His day were

2. Why you should choose Jesus to be *your* authority

3. How "sons of God" live in our age of darkness—what they value, how they think, and what they do.

4. What God has planned for His sons both in this life and in the next

Throughout this Sermon Jesus presses the point that His Father is creating a kingdom of sons of light to invade, lighten, and conquer darkness for all eternity.

Join us in this exciting study to learn all it means to be a son of God, to be *all in* for God "so that you may be sons of your Father in heaven."

Kay

PRECEPTS FOR LIFE

with Kay Arthur

™

PRECEPTS FOR LIFE™
Study Guide

This Bible study material was designed for use with the TV and Radio teaching program, Precepts for Life™ with renowned Bible study teacher Kay Arthur, a production of Precept Ministries International. This inductive 30-minute daily Bible study program airs on many satellite, cable, and broadcast stations, and on the internet at **www.preceptsforlife.com.**

As with all Inductive Bible studies, the best way to use the material is to complete the assignments in each lesson before listening or watching the PFL program for that day. These programs are also available on DVD and CD at **www.preceptsforlife.com** or by phone (1.800.763.1990 for television viewers or 1.800.734.7707 for radio listeners). For more information about the Precept Inductive Bible Study Method and Precept Ministries International, visit **www.preceptsforlife.com.**

These materials are also useful for Bible study apart from the Precepts for Life™ programs. We hope you'll find them valuable for studying God's Word and that your walk will be strengthened by the life-changing Truth you'll encounter each day.

Sermon on the Mount STUDY GUIDE
Published by Precept Ministries of Reach Out, Inc.
P. O. Box 182218
Chattanooga, TN 37422

ISBN–13: 978-1-62119-451-4

PROGRAM 1 — When Heaven Touched Earth

TODAY'S TEXTS

Matthew 28:16-20
1:1
1:21-23
2:1-2
3:1-2
3:11-17
4:1-9
4:17-23
5:1-12

1. Read Matthew 28:16-20.

   a. What does Jesus tell His disciples to do before He ascends into heaven?

   b. Is it important for us to learn "all He commanded" in order to teach it to all nations?

2. What do we learn about Jesus and His kingdom that we should teach from the following verses?

   a. Matthew 1:1: Who did the Messiah descend from?

   b. Matthew 1:21: Why will the "Son" be called "Jesus"?

   c. Matthew 1:22-23

      1) What does "Immanuel" mean?

      2) What does this tell us about Jesus? Is he just another prophet?

   d. Matthew 2:1-2

      1) What particular title of Jesus is a threat to Herod?

      2) What did the wise men come to do and what does this tell us about Jesus?

   e. Matthew 4:1-9

      1) Where did the descending Spirit "lead" Jesus after He was baptized—to fame and fortune?

      2) What does man "live by"?

   f. Matthew 5:1-12: List the godly characteristics Jesus attaches "blessed" to:

PROGRAM 2 — You Can Know Heaven's Yours

TODAY'S TEXTS

Matthew 5:1-12
Isaiah 6:1-7
John 5:19
Isaiah 57:15; 66:1-2
Luke 5:1-8
Romans 7:24-25
12:3-8
3:10, 11, 20

CROSS REFERENCES

Matthew 5:20
Romans 5:18
1 Corinthians 1:30
Philippians 3:9
John 5:19

1. Review the beatitudes in Matthew 5:1-12 marking the blessings God correlated with specific godly characteristics with a purple underline.

2. See **Cross-reference** Matthew 5:20.

   a. Are the godly characteristics listed in the Sermon on the Mount optional for believers?

   b. Whose righteousness are we ultimately saved by? (See **Cross-references** Romans 5:18, 1 Corinthians 1:30, and Philippians 3:9.)

3. What does "poor in spirit" (5:3) mean?

   a. How does this contrast with "poor in flesh"? Can a person be rich in flesh and poor in spirit? Rich in spirit but poor in flesh?

   b. Generally, are there different kinds of poverty and wealth?

4. Read Isaiah 57:15 and 66:1-2.

   a. What kind of person does God "dwell with"? Is this an external action or an internal attitude connected to all actions?

   b. What specific attitude toward His Word does God commend? Should we take God's Word "lightly"? (Recall Jesus' words about what we "live" on.)

PROGRAM 3 — Submit Your Power Under God's Control

TODAY'S TEXTS
Matthew 5:5
Psalm 103:19
Numbers 12:1-13
Matthew 11:28-30
Psalm 37:1-11, 22
2 Corinthians 12:7-10

1. Read Matthew 5:5. How will the "gentle" be blessed?

2. Now read Numbers 12:1-13.
   a. What did Miriam and Aaron complain about with respect to Moses?
   b. What three ways did the Lord contrast Moses with ordinary "prophets"?

      1) _____

      2) _____

      3) _____

3. Now read Matthew 11:28-30.
   a. What kinds of people is Jesus inviting to Himself?
   b. What does He promise them (vv. 28, 29)?

4. Finally, read 2 Corinthians 12:7-10.
   a. What did God give Paul to keep him from boasting?
   b. How did the Lord respond to Paul's request? What did He say about the relationship between power and weakness?

PROGRAM 4 — What Does True Christianity Look Like?

TODAY'S TEXTS
Matthew 7:21; 5:6
Romans 3:10
John 4:10-14; 7:37-39; 6:35
Isaiah 55:1-2
Psalm 42:1-2; 63:1
Matthew 5:7; 18:33
James 2:12-13

CROSS REFERENCES
Isaiah 29:13
Matthew 15:8

1. What do the following verses tell you about hungering and/or thirsting for righteousness?
   a. Matthew 5:6

   b. Romans 3:10

   c. John 4:10-14

   d. John 7:37-39

   e. Psalm 42:1-2

2. Now read Matthew 5:7 and 18:33 in its context (vv. 21-35).
   a. Why are the merciful "blessed"?

   b. What did the unmerciful servant do to his servant? What can we apply from this parable to our own lives?

3. Finally, read James 2:12-13.
   a. How should we "speak and act" according to James' teaching?

   b. What kind of judgment comes on those who have shown no mercy?

PROGRAM 5 — We Are the Salt & the Light—Therefore Persecution is Coming

TODAY'S TEXTS

Matthew 5:9-12
Isaiah 9:6-7
Luke 12:49-53
Matthew 28:18-20
2 Corinthians 5:17-20
Matthew 5:11-12
23:29-30
Hebrews 11:24-40
2 Timothy 3:12-13
4:6-8, 16-18

CROSS REFERENCES

2 Thessalonians 1:5-10
John 5:29
Matthew 26:56
Hebrews 13:5-6

1. **Peace.** Read the listed verses and then answer the questions.

    a. Matthew 5:9-12.

        1) Are sons of God peacemakers by definition?

        2) Why are they, then, reviled, persecuted, and insulted?

    b. Luke 12:49-53.

        1) Did the Prince of Peace come to bring peace into our evil world?

        2) Why does the peace He brings cause division and where?

2. **Persecution.** Read the listed verses and answer the questions.

    a. Matthew 5:11-12.

        1) Why should we rejoice when we're persecuted according to Jesus?

        2) What is "persecution"—what are we persecuted *for?*

    b. 2 Timothy 4:6-8, 16-18.

        1) List Paul's three perspectives on his ministry life (look for 3 "the"s).

        2) What was "laid up" for him as the result?

PROGRAM 6 | What Does Jesus Say About the Law?

TODAY'S TEXTS
Matthew 5:13-20
Romans 8:1-6
Matthew 5:21-22

CROSS REFERENCES
John 1:5
Galatians 5:16

1. Read Matthew 5:13-20.

    a. What do you think *"salt of the earth"* is? (Some have suggested fertilizer rather than Sodium Chloride.) In any case, what is Jesus' main point? What are we to be and what are we to avoid?

    b. According to v. 17, what is Jesus' relationship to "the Law and the Prophets"?

2. Now read Romans 8:1-6.

    a. Are any who are "in Christ" condemned?

    b. Why not? What has the Spirit done?

    c. Explain the contrast "What the Law *could* not do . . . God *did.*"

3. Finally, read Matthew 5:21-22.

    a. Explain Jesus' contrast between "the ancients were told" and "I say to you."

    b. Is anger with a brother ever justified? What does Jesus threaten to those who express their anger with generalities like "good for nothing" and "fool"?

PROGRAM 7 | The Heart's Relationship to the Law

TODAY'S TEXTS
Matthew 5:21-48; 18:8

CROSS REFERENCES
1 Corinthians 15:37-38, 50

Read Matthew 5:21-48.

1. Are murder and anger related? How dangerous are our words according to Jesus?

2. Should we "write off" brothers we owe debts to and then sacrifice to the Lord? What should we do first? What does Jesus threaten if we don't?

3. Is adultery physical only? Do you think Jesus is telling us to cut off *physical* body parts (eyes, hands) that cause us to sin or cut off our *lusting spirits* from these parts so we don't use them to act?

4. What one exception does Jesus permit divorce for?

5. What practical commands does Jesus offer with respect to:

    a. Strict "eye-for-eye" justice?

    b. Literally getting struck by someone?

    c. Loan collateral (in His day, sometimes an article of clothing)?

PROGRAM 8	Beware of Practicing Righteousness Before Men

TODAY'S TEXTS

Matthew 6:1-18

CROSS-REFERENCES

Matthew 26:44

2 Corinthians 12:8

Matthew 18:21-35

2 Samuel 1:12; 12:16

Psalm 35:13

1. Review Matthew 6:1-18.

   a. What is the consequence of the motive of practicing righteousness to be seen by men?

   b. What do "hypocrites" do? What do you think Jesus meant by "they have their reward in full"? Is this an eternal reward?

   c. How can we give "in secret"? What promise comes with this?

   d. Contrast the two kinds of praying.

   e. What does "meaningless repetition" mean? Didn't Jesus and Paul repeat prayers three times? (See **Cross-References** Matthew 26:44 and 2 Corinthians 12:8.)

   f. Is forgiveness important according to verses 12 and 14? Read **Cross-Reference** Matthew 18:21-35. Why should we forgive others? Give as many reasons as you can find in the texts.

   g. Contrast the two ways to fast (vv. 16-18).

PROGRAM 9	Are You Worried? Your Heavenly Father Says Do Not Be Anxious!

TODAY'S TEXTS

Matthew 6:19-34

1 Timothy 6:6-10

Mark 4:1-9, 14-20

CROSS-REFERENCES

Isaiah 5:20

Psalm 90:10

Galatians 1:10

Philippians 4:19

1. Read Matthew 6:19-24.

   a. What are three good reasons for not storing up treasures on earth but, rather, storing up treasures in heaven?

   b. Is there any connection between what we value (treasure) and our inner life?

   c. How does our inner attitude and outward service treat two masters? Why?

2. Now read 1 Timothy 6:6-10.

   a. What do the combination of godliness and contentment produce?

   b. What three factors related to the desire to be rich plunge men into ruin and destruction?

3. Now read Matthew 6:25-34. Summarize the various reasons why we should not be anxious.

4. Let's wrap it up by reviewing Matthew 6:33-34.

   a. What does Jesus tell us to seek "first" in our lives? What promise comes with this priority?

   b. What one last reason does He give for not being anxious about the future? How is this helpful for you?

PROGRAM 10

When God Said Do Not Judge, What Did He Mean?

TODAY'S TEXTS
Matthew 7:1-29

CROSS-REFERENCES
Isaiah 5:20

Read Matthew 7:1-29.

1. vv. 1-5: How do we know from these verses what kind of judgment, negative or positive, Jesus is focusing on?

2. v. 6: Can I know a "swine" in advance if I've had no experience with him or her?

3. vv. 7-12:

   a. What does Jesus promise to those who ask, seek, and knock?

   b. How does He encourage you to ask based on the normal relationship between a child and father?

4. vv. 13-27 Hypocrisy:

   a. Describe the two "gate"s and the people who pass through them. Does this truth make us more dependent on the Lord? If so, how?

   b. Can a good tree produce bad fruit or a bad tree good fruit? What, then, are we "looking for" in people—long-term consistency between what and what?

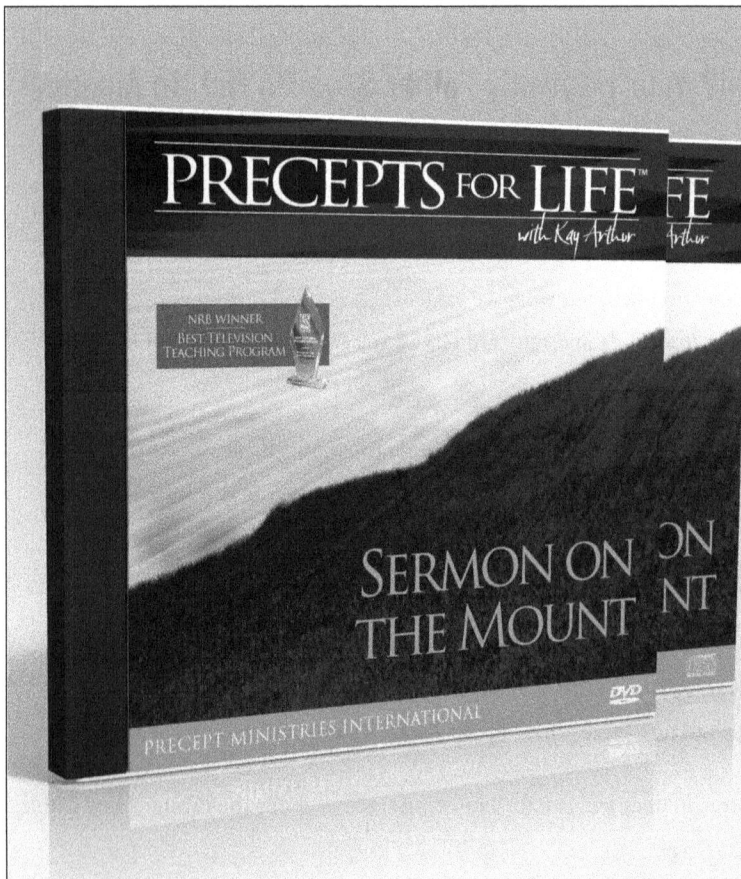

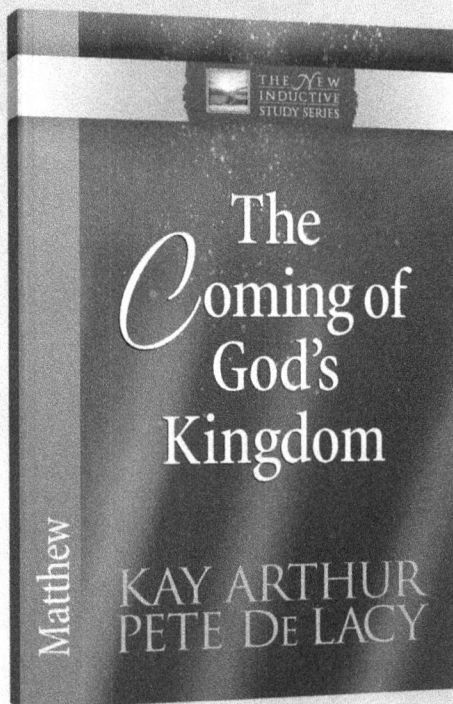

Did you know...

that you can walk more closely with God by studying with others? People are meeting in small group studies and church Sunday school classes in all 50 states—and there's probably one near you. Want to join them?

Find a group near you—TV viewers call 1.800.763.1990, radio listeners call 1.888.734.7707, or visit www. PreceptsForLife.com.

Let us hear from you!

Have you been blessed by the teachings on *Precepts For Life*™? We'd love to hear your story.

Visit www.PreceptsForLife.com and click "Contact Us." Or write to:

Precepts For Life
P. O. Box 182218
Chattanooga, TN 37422.

Make sure to mention the call letters of the station where you tune in.

DISCOVER TRUTH FOR YOURSELF

Our passion is for you to discover Truth for yourself through Inductive Bible Study—a unique Bible study method you'll discover in the following pages and use throughout this study, as we engage this important topic together verse by verse.

You can't do a better thing than sit at Jesus' feet, listening to His every word. God's Word, the Bible, has answers for every situation you'll face in life. Listen to what God is saying to you, face-to-face, with truth to transform your life!

INDUCTIVE BIBLE STUDY METHOD

To study and understand God's Word, we use the Inductive Bible Study Method at Precept Ministries International. The Bible is our main source of truth. Before looking for insights from people and commentaries *about* the Bible, we get into the Word of God, beginning with observing the text.

❶ Observation

This is a very interactive process, well worth the time because the truths you discover for yourself will be accurate and profound. It begins by asking the five W and H questions.

Who is speaking? Who is this about? Who are the main characters? And to whom is the speaker speaking?

What subjects and/or events are covered in the chapter? What do you learn about the people, the events, and the teachings from the text? What instructions are given?

When did or will the events recorded occur?

Where did or will this happen? Where was it said?

Why is something said? Why will an event occur? Why this time, person, and/or place?

How will it happen? How will it be done? How is it illustrated?

Careful observation leads to interpretation—discovering what the text means.

❷ Interpretation

The more you observe, the greater you'll understand God's Word. Since Scripture is the best interpreter of Scripture, you and I will be looking at contexts and cross-references to enhance our understanding of the meaning of God's message.

Where should observation and interpretation lead? Application.

❸ Application

After we've observed the text and discovered what it means, we need to think and live accordingly. The result is a transformed life—the more you and I are in the Word of God and adjusting our thinking and behavior to its precepts for life, the more we are changed into the likeness of Jesus Christ! He is the living Word of God who became flesh, the Savior of the world, our coming King of kings!

SO WHERE DO YOU BEGIN?

The Bible is *God's* book, His Word, so when you study it you need to seek the Author's help. Begin with prayer, asking God to lead you into all truth, then open the Study Companion. (We suggest you work one program ahead of the broadcast to get the most out of the study.) Look at the general layout of each day's program and you will find the following:

- Introduction—usually with a challenging question
- Questions that contain pointers on using the Inductive Bible Study Method
- **Where's That Verse?** section containing the Primary Study Passage and several cross-references related to the topic
- Concluding Prayer

WHAT'S NEXT?

- In some programs, I'll point out key words to mark. You'll find many of them on the back cover of this Study Companion with *suggested* colors and symbols to spot them quickly in the text. Color coding key words helps you identify and recall. We have included a cutout bookmark so you can remember to mark each key word the same way throughout the text.

  You can mark these key words before or after the program, whichever is easier. You can also get the CD or DVD of the program and mark the key words later while studying.

Feel free to mark them your own way—there's nothing sacred about the particular symbols and colors I use!

- The cross-references I mention in these programs are under **Where's That Verse?** After you read them, you can jot them in the margins of the **Observation Worksheets** or write them in the wide margins of your Bible. I suggest you first pencil them in, then write them in ink later.

- For book studies, you'll find an **At A Glance** chart in the back. After we complete a chapter, record a summary theme there and in the space provided in your **Observation Worksheets**. Themes help you remember main ideas of chapters **At A Glance** after you finish the study. You'll also find these charts after each book in the *New Inductive Study Bible*.

MISSED A PROGRAM?

- Go to our website at **www.PreceptsForLife.com**. TV viewers can call 1.800.763.1990 and radio listeners 1.888.734.7707 to learn how to find programs online.

GETTING THE MOST FROM THIS STUDY

- Try to stay one program ahead of me so you'll learn directly from the Word of God and our time together will be like a "discussion group," as we reason together through the Scriptures. You'll get much more out of our time together if you've done this preparation.

- Try to memorize a key verse for every program covered. God will bring these to your remembrance when you need them!

- Pray about what you learn each day. Ask God to remind you of these truths and give you another person to share them with. These two exercises will do amazing things in your life.

- Get the CD or DVD set of this series and listen when you get ready for work in the morning, do chores around the house, or have family devotions. Or listen with an open Bible and discuss the teaching and its application to your life. Get together with a friend, view or listen to a message, and discuss it or use it for family devotions. You can also view or listen programs online. Visit **www.PreceptsForLife.com.**

- Request Precept's mailings to stay abreast of what God is doing around the world and to pray for the needs we share with you. You can be a significant part of this unique global ministry God is using to establish people in His Word. Here are some items you can request:

- The *Plumbline*—Precept Ministry's monthly e-newsletter that keeps you up to date on Bible study topics, products and events that help you in your walk with Christ.

- A prayer list so you can partner with us in prayer for our ministries in nearly 150 countries and 70 languages.

- "Inside information" each month when you join our "E-Team" of regular prayer and financial supporters. Visit **www.PreceptsForLife.com** for more information on how you can support our programs. (You can check out the current monthly letter right now on our website.)

- Advance notice of conferences at our headquarters in Chattanooga and throughout the United States and Canada.

- Information about our study tours in Israel, Jordan, Greece, Turkey, and Italy, where we teach various books of the Bible right where the action occurred!

• We use one of the most accurate translations of the Bible, the New American Standard (Updated). If the topic is a book study, our **Observation Worksheets** will contain the complete text. Since you'll be instructed to mark words and phrases and make notes in the text, you'll want to have colored pencils or pens available. As you grow in inductive study skills, you may want to use your Bible instead. We believe the best Bible to use is the *New Inductive Study Bible*. See our back pages to find out more about this ultimate study Bible. Now get started!

• Finally, stay in touch with me personally. I'd so love to hear from you by email or letter so I can be sensitive to where you are and what you're experiencing—problems you're wrestling with, questions you have, etc. This will help me teach more effectively and personally. Just email us at info@precept.org. (Don't worry, Beloved, I won't mention you by name; but as you listen, you'll know I've heard you!)

I'm committed to you . . . because of Him. The purpose of the "Precepts For Life" TV & Radio programs is to help you realize your full potential in God, so you can become the exemplary believer God intends you to be…studying the Bible inductively, viewing the world biblically, making disciples intentionally, and serving the Church faithfully in the power of the Holy Spirit."

That's my vision for us as believers! Won't you help us spread it to others?

Looking for people…looking for truth!

How Do I Start Studying The Bible?

Do you wonder,
God, how can I obey You and study your Word? Where do I begin? How can I discover truth for myself?

DISCOVER TRUTH FOR YOURSELF

There are some study tools we would recommend for you to begin with, as each will teach you the inductive method of study. By inductive we mean that you can go straight to the Word of God and discover truth for yourself, so you can say … "for You, Yourself have taught me" (Psalm 119:102).

Let's Get Started! For a jump start on inductive study, we recommend the following:

- *Lord, Teach Me To Study The Bible in 28 Days.* In this hands-on introduction to the basics of inductive study, you'll see why you need to study God's Word and how to dig into the truths of a book of the Bible. The instructions will walk you through the books of Jonah and Jude, and you'll be awed at what you see on your own! Discussion questions are included.

- *God, Are You There? Do You Care? Do You Know About Me?* This 13-week, self-contained inductive study on the Gospel of John is powerful and life-changing. Study the book of John, as you learn and put into practice inductive study skills. The Gospel of John was written that you might believe that Jesus is the Son of God and that believing, might have life in His name. You will know you are loved! Discussion questions are included.

- *How to Study Old Testament History and Prophecy Workshop.* Discover truths about who God is and how He works as you learn to study inductively, step by step, and be challenged to apply these truths to your life. This workshop will give you the tools to study and understand Old Testament history and prophecy. Go to www.precept.org or call 800-763-8280 to find out about workshops in your area, or online training.

- *How to Study a New Testament Letter Workshop.* Grow in the knowledge of the Lord Jesus Christ and His plan for your life. This inductive study workshop will equip you to study the New Testament letters and apply their truths to your life. Go to www.precept. org or call 800-763-8280 to find out about workshops in your area, or online training.

Now that you've begun . . . continue studying inductively using one of these:

- *40 Minute Bible Studies.* These 6-week topical studies are a good for personal study and a great way to start discipling others one-on-one or in a group setting—teaching them who God is, introducing them to Jesus Christ, and helping them learn God's precepts for life. These studies enable you to discover what God says about different issues of life. No homework is necessary for the students prior to group time.

- *The New Inductive Study Series,* now complete covering every book of the Bible, was created to help you discover truth for yourself and go deeper into God's precepts, promises and purposes. This powerful series is ideal for personal study, small groups, Sunday school classes, family devotions, and discipling others. Containing 13-week long studies, the New Inductive Study Series also provides easy planning for church curriculum! You can now survey the entire Bible

- *Lord Series.* These life-changing devotional studies cover in greater depth major issues of our relationship with God and with others, teaching us how to practically live out our faith. Ideal for small groups, these contain discussion guides and teaching DVDs are available for some.

- *Discover 4 Yourself* is a dynamic series of inductive studies for children. Children who can read learn how to discover truth for themselves through the life-impacting skills of observation, interpretation, and application. You'll be amazed at the change that comes when children know for themselves what the Word of God says! Teach them now so they can stand firm in a first-hand knowledge of truth as they hit their teen years. This award-winning series is popular in Christian schools and among homeschoolers. Teacher's guides are available online.

- *The New Inductive Study Bible (NISB)* is a unique and exciting! Most study Bibles give you someone else's interpretation of the text. The NISB doesn't tell you what to believe, rather it helps you discover truth for yourself by showing you how to study inductively and providing instructions, study helps, and application questions for each book of the Bible, as well as wide margins for your notes. It's filled with many wonderful features that will guide you toward the joy of discovering the truths of God's Word for yourself. This Bible is your legacy.

GO DEEPER WITH OTHERS...
IN SMALL GROUP BIBLE STUDIES

Join others in the study of God's Word, sharing insights from the Scripture and discussing application to your life. Each of the studies described above are appropriate for groups as well as for individual study.

Discussion questions are included, so that you can dialogue about what you're learning with a group. These studies will teach you what it means to live by God's Word—and how it is applied to life. Learn about and discuss with others the truth that sets you free! To find out about inductive Bible study groups in your area, go to www.precept.org or call 800-763-8280.

DISCIPLE

How can you help others study God's Word inductively? Use the studies described above to share with others—one-on-one or in a small group. Lead others in discovering truth for themselves and experience the joy of seeing God change lives!

If you want training in how to lead these and other Precept Upon Precept studies go to www.precept.org or call us at 800-763-8280.

**Precept Ministries International | P.O. Box 182218 | Chattanooga, TN 37422
800.763.8280 | www.precept.org**